Reflections

by A.H-Rooms

TGBTG

The giver of the gift

Acknowledgements

First and foremost, I would like to acknowledge
the Lord for his strength and guidance. Without
Him, my gift would not be mine.

I would like to thank all those that have
contributed to the making of this book with their
love, support and words.

Thank you to all those that continue to support
me and those that have purchased my books
'Vintage' and 'Hugs'.

I thank you all greatly.

I pray you enjoy Reflections.

Truly yours,

A. H-Rooms

X

Contents

Love Is

The fragrance
of your love yet lingers.

Gone
yet you remain.

Aware of your presence
reassures my heart and,
I Smile.

I Very Nearly Broke

I very nearly broke.

I can't help visiting that place!
It has cost much to
live next door,
or nearer still.

There are no doors.
I am awake.
The walls are thin.
Thread bare
keeps me adrift
there seems no shore.

Fiery fierce are the tides.
The waves are high.
The night is deep.
Be still my soul.
One day
we will
find rest.

A Prisoner of...

A prisoner of ones pain,
oh no!

Within are gems which offer
blessings
gives one wings.

Strength
to soar new heights
and be renewed.

Dear Silence

Pause.
Be still.

In its Presence
quietly one waits.

Holy this moment
as He is ushered in.
Inviting us to His bosom,
what a blessing!

Silenced by this meeting.
All other concerns
are gone.
Bask in this fullness
of
The Eternal One.

This moment of silence.
Such graciousness and awe.
Our hearts bow in worship
for,
He is here.

Never

Never to touch
or hold again.
Opportunities once had,
chose to let go.

Oh bring back those days!
To better ones best.

No more mask to hide behind.
For better tomorrow,
another chance.

Place Me

Place me
'neath your wings
so I will not fall.

Place me there
so I can be near you.

Place me where I can rest.
Content at last
at the sound of
life's rhythm…
your heart

Place me there
to worship and adore…
You.

I Tossed and Turned

I tossed and turned.
Could not stop.
Couldn't rest.
Searched.
Could not find.

Then
quietly
one day
exhausted with myself
a voice called my name.
Yes Lord.
Master.
Come in
and take
your place.

I now know
by His love
and grace
what is perfect
rest.

Moments

Moments of splendours
spent with you.

Make life worth
living again and
again.

Moments of…
Just
With
you.

Tell Me Anything

Tell me anything.
Tell me a lie.
Just tell me anything.
For anything will do.
Anything you tell me
will be true.

That way I wouldn't have to think
for I'll just keep on believing
just any old thing.
I'll keep on pretending the promises
you made
when you told me
we would forever live.

Just tell me.
Tell me anything.
Tell me a lie.
That way I will pretend
it has soothed my heart.

All hurt will subside
but in the meantime
I will pretend I believe your lie.

Towards

A last tear.
A quiet thought.
A final word.
A wave goodbye
to yesteryears
and a smile of anticipation
that will
in meeting
wipe away
all tears.

A Surrendered Soul

Here I am Lord.
All I was
am
and yet to be.

Fickle and restless.
Pained and broken.
Near crushed.

Wanting
yet fearing.
Though
loving in a sort of way
yet needing more of Thee
and offering
on the way
to Thee
a surrendered soul.

Friend

You tried to tell us
you could not stay.

We will remember and
mourn our loss of you.

Great friend.
Rest sweet.

We Nearly Made It

We nearly made it.
You and I.
We very nearly did.

A love so strong
that lasted through
the test of time.
We very nearly made it.

But this love
was never meant to be.
It never really was.
Lust has a way
of holding on.
Wanting to belong.

We very nearly made it.
Things seemed so right.
So sure.

Yet somehow
the signs were
always there tho
many seemed not to
have known it.

So goodbye to a
seeming type of
friendship.

Not all was bad.
The pain of reminiscence
will pass.
As will the tears.

When healing comes
we'll both be glad
that fate was kind
to ensure that
we never really made it.

Bind My Heart

Bind my heart to Thine.
Make it all Thy own.
Bind yet stricter still.
Thy love alone to hold.

Bind my heart to Thine.
To be Thine and
Thine alone.
Ever to keep me near
for fickle are my ways.

Bind my heart to Thine.
In Thine sublime ecstasy
I rest in Thee.

Bind
entwine my heart.
May it ever be
just Thine.

Just Far Enough

Looking up
I realise that I'm under
home sky.

It's only with my feet on the ground
that I feel in another's land.

Sometimes even around
seems homely and familiar.

I'm not far away.
Just far enough
from home.

Silent

Silent ecstasy.
You
look at me
through me.
I look at you
through you.

We meet
and rest.

Silent
ecstasy.

Witness

I was a witness
to your silent screams.
Your empty gaze drew my eyes
to your burning flames
that could not be extinguished.
You made me a witness to your pain.
Forever entwined.

May You

May you
go into
the night
blessed and
protected.

May the dawn
meet you
refreshed
and reawakened
ready to meet
the day.

Forever

Lord
Thou art forever
my safe place.

May I find
my rest
in Thee.

Let My Heart Sing

Let my heart
sing aloud
with gladness.

Let my heart
sing with
joyous acclaim
to Him.
The King of Kings.

My heart Sings
to The One Who was and Is
and forever the same.

Beyond

I love you beyond everyone and
everything.
Beyond where I know
and
where I can find
and
far beyond where I can think
or imagine
and
I love you more.

She Can

She can cope
all alone.
She will cope
all alone.

She needs no help.
Manages well.
Looks all right.
All is well.
She can cope
and she is doing well.

Perhaps I should
offer some help?
Ask if there's anything?
No!

She can hope.
No need to offer any help.
Maybe
She
might
need
rest?

A little break?
A breath?
No.
She can cope.
Everyone says so.
No one else has offered.
So it must be so that
she can cope.
One certainly hopes so.

I tossed and turned
and couldn't rest.
Why then so restless?
When we all agreed
she can cope and is doing so well.

We received a call.
Someone had to break down the door
and carried her out.
Everyone watched, shocked.

Cannot Cease

Cannot cease.
Cannot die.
This love of Thine
that comes from
on high.

O love divine
shared to mankind.
Thy gift of love and offering
beyond all price.
Your ultimate sacrifice.

With yet a pleading heart
you bid us
come.

Hold Me

Hold me
closely
softly
tightly.
I want to be held.
Please, just, hold me.

Cannot

Cannot lose you.
Cannot see you.
Be with you.
Can only hope and dream.
Never to touch
hold
or
share.

Cannot sleep.
Cannot eat.
Drifting.
Drifting.
Drifting
slowly into oblivion.

Cannot live.
Cannot die.
Without you.

But

If you were to love me
as I do you
we could
be one
or visa versa?

No Regrets

No regrets
of what we had
and what we might have been.
No regrets
of our love and laughter.
Evening strolls.
Morning calls.
No regrets.

No regrets
of shared sunshine.
Golden moments
of moonlight streets on
dark nights.
No regrets.

No regrets
of the look in your eyes
when yours
met mine.
No regrets.

I Carry You

I carry you
for
you are mine.
Exchange your
struggle
for my rest.

Enjoy life's journey.
It's a gift for sure.
Challenges are
surmountable
for I'm taking
you through.

Remember my child
I am
your
home.

Weakness

Lord
in my weakness
be my almighty
strength.
I withstand all
and every will of the enemy.
Always
I want
desire
and need
your love.
All honour and glory
to Thee.
Now and forever.

Songs

Songs of
praise
and thanksgiving
to our Lord and King
will defeat
the enemy.

The Loving Touch

The loving touch
as you passed
by
has left the fragrance
of
your presence
and it's embrace.

In The Shadows
Of The Night

In the shadows of the night
your love reached out
and embraced me
kept me so safe
beneath your
wings.

I am loved,
so loved.
Comforted and stilled,
to rest in your Presence.

I am blessed,
so blessed.
To always have your love.
For all times and all eternity,
Thank You Lord.

Love Is Forever

Love is a duty
and responsibility.
Love is everything divine
Love is God.

It Was

Just one careless,
carefree kiss
it was to be.
We didn.t even care.
Not him,
not me.
And then the force
of habit came
in time.
He never really asked me
to be his.
I didn't want him
to be mine.
But as if within a
quick flash it
seemed to be.
One day it just happened
as if always meant to be.
That careless
carefree kiss we stole,
sealed us.
Him and me.

Remember

Remember the past
and learn its lessons.
Remember today
when it becomes yesterday.
Now do your best,
look forward to tomorrow
with hope and love
always to be rebirthed.

A Suicide Note

A view.
A gin.
Go out
in a swing.
They will continue
to remember
all I once did.

Love Me

Love me not to change me
but that more of me
I'll be.

Defend

To be able to
defend
one must
always be prepared.

Your Tapestry

Your tapestry
of love
fills my heart
with gladness
and delight.

Loved, Treasured

Loved.
Treasured.
Remembered.

Through each journey
you remain.
Carried through fore bearings.
Steadfast.
Instructed by life's lessons.
Chiselled
for a greater good.

Searched into.
Step forward.
The gem awaits
your rediscovering.

Each journey
takes one nearer home.

Continue

Continue doing to me
the things you do.
Only if you yourself
will like it done
to you.

No Bridges

And yet I waited.
If only for the occasional pause.
Amidst the rush
a smile of recognition
now and then.
A thank you of
Appreciation.
A touch to comfort.
Word to heal.
Yet,
one waited.

Misunderstood.
Perhaps we thought
but the tide of time
had passed.

No more surging forth.
There were
no bridges built.
One waits no more.

His Chair

His chair is still in the corner
where he once sat
ate,
drank,
slept,
laughed.

His chair is still in the corner
by the fireside
where he once
stared into its flames
as though in a mediative
trance.

His chair is still in the corner
like a memorial plaque.

His chair is still in the corner
but he won't be coming back.

Perfect Love

Tenderly embrace me
in spite of my waywardness.
Shield,
Support,
Sustain,
and nurture me
unjudgmentally.
So unfailingly
you dried every tear
and drew me near.

Oh perfect love
I surrender.

Just Over There

Just over there.
Beyond those hills.
In the valley below
not far from the sea.
Along the quiet lanes
where life is no strain.
Where the rustling of leaves
and the bird are all tuned.
Where I've many times
hummed, walked and smiled in glee.

Over there I gazed
at their cribs.
Just over there.
Just over there.

Allow Me

Allow me
to continue to be drunk
from the nectar of your
love.

Missed Moments

We could have shared our
moments more
as we had done
sometimes before.

When love
was young
and we drank
off its joy.

Why couldn't our love
grow from its source.

Missed moments
never to be returned.

Hunger

Although seems filled.
In need for more.
Nothing suffices
the thirst and hunger
to fill the void within.

Tried to fill myself
with favourite things.
Laughter,
song,
dance,
friends,
food.
However ,
nothing will fill the
space within.

Come quickly Lord
into my life
and reign
my Lord
and King.

Sincerely Yours

Sincerely yours
for all time.
Oh please be mine
for I am yours.

Grant Me

Grant me
a heart of
gladness
joy
gratitude
and thanks.
Amen.

Preparation

Time spent in
preparation
counted as
great gain.

Empty

Fill my void and
empty spaces Lord
with Thy self
for
I am
famished.

You Promised

You promised.

Yet
as one came close
to your embrace
you withdrew.

The Joy Of Living

In the ecstasy of the afternoon
sunlight
two flies
danced
kissed
playfully
in mid-air.

Walk Beside Me Lord

Walk beside me Lord.
Please hold my hand
through darker
pathways.
Let me not stray.
Undeserving
yet boldly
I ask for your grace
from day to day.
Walk with me,
Lord.

I Love You

I love you
because
you allow me
to be
yet love me
as I am
for who I am
and yet
to become.

Touch Me

Touch me with your kind thoughts.
Soft words.
Listening ears.
Sharing hands.
Embracing arms
and
eyes that say
'I understand'.

Touch me
and
make me whole.

I Reached Out From Life's Darkness

I reached out from life's
darkness and you were already there.
I called out but
you had already answered.
In my longings
you had already
met all my needs.
When I looked within
You oh Lord was already there.

I Found It In You

That very moment
when you looked
into my eyes
the answer to my
dreams and prayers
was found.

Mame

Mame held me close
and danced
an ancestral dance
she didn't think I remembered.

The next time we met
there were no more springs in her
steps
nor songs on her lips.

For we knew
it was time.

Treasure

The treasure of my life
is found in
you.

Come Dance

Come dance again
with me my lovely.
Come swing the way
we used to long ago.
Come allow us to
share again.

A moment
that
will last eternally.

Come
let's dance.

Give thanks to the Lord
for he is good.
His love endures forever.

Psalm 136:1